Facebook:
Master Facebook
Marketing
Facebook Advertising, Small Business & Branding

without the consent of the author or copyright owner. Legal action will be pursued if this is breached.

Disclaimer Notice:

Please note the information contained within this document is for educational and entertainment purposes only. Every attempt has been made to provide accurate, up to date and reliable complete information. No warranties of any kind are expressed or implied. Readers acknowledge that the author is not engaging in the rendering of legal, financial, medical or professional advice.

By reading this document, the reader agrees that under no circumstances are we responsible for any losses, direct or indirect, which are incurred as a result of the use of information contained within this document, including, but not limited to, —errors, omissions, or inaccuracies.

Table of Contents

Free Bonus!!!

We would like to offer you our FREE Guide to jump start you on a path to improve your life & Exclusive access to our Breakthrough Book Club!!! It's a place where we offer a NEW FREE E-book every week! Also our members are actively discussing, reviewing, and sharing their thoughts on the Book of The Week and on topics to help each other Breakthrough Life's Obstacles! Please Enjoy Your FREE Guide & Access to the Breakthrough Book Club

INTRODUCTION:

Facebook is practically all over the place – and practically just about everyone is on it. This makes Facebook one of the best places to promote your business or brand. But it isn't as simple as going in Facebook and selling stuff or promoting your business agenda.

It takes a certain skillset or savvy.

In this book, I'll show you how to promote or market your brand or business on Facebook the right way. Specifically, I'll show you how to do so for free and using Facebook's paid advertisements. Doing things the Facebook way can significantly increase your chances of successfully promoting your brand or business via Facebook – and consequently, enjoy good revenue.

So what are you waiting for? Turn the page and let's begin!

CHAPTER 1
FACEBOOK MARKETING

Without a doubt, the largest platform for social media in the history of the world – and probably the universe, assuming we're the only intelligent life forms around – is Facebook. If you're still one of the naysayers and heretics of the humongous social media empire, consider the following facts as of 20 September 2015 from the reputable website statisticbrain.com:

- There are about 1.44 billion – yes, billion – active Facebook accounts every month;

- There are about 874 million active Facebook users on mobile devices;

- Facebook's membership base grew by 12% in 2015;

- A total of 640 million man-hours were spent on Facebook;

- Close to half – or about 48% of total Facebook users log in daily;

- Each visit on Facebook takes about 18 minutes on average; and

- There are over 74 million Facebook pages.

If you're still a doubter as to the immensity and influence of Facebook after these facts and figures, chances are you'll forever be one.

Now regardless of how these figures are presented, one thing is clear – there's a lot of people using Facebook. If it were a place, it'll be the most populated place on earth. And what does that mean for you as an entrepreneur or a marketing professional? That's right – prospects! With more prospects come greater business opportunities, eh?

FACEBOOK SENSE IS COMMON SENSE

While it's a given that not all the people on Facebook can be your actual prospects, even a tiny portion of the pie can still mean huge revenues for you. That being said, Facebook's ginormous size implies that it's the best place to market your products over the Internet. But wait – there's more, as this is just the tip of the proverbial Internet marketing iceberg. Here other reasons to justify that using Facebook to market your product or service makes perfect sense.

Segments

Here's a very cool and marketing-related piece of Facebook information: Facebook maintains a gigantic database that contains tons of useful marketing information about its users such as age, location, likes, favorites and interests, among others. Now what's that supposed to mean?

Ok, hear me out. You can advertise your brand or business on Facebook in 2 different ways: free and paid advertising. The information I mentioned earlier is of particular importance to the latter – paid advertising.

Why, you may ask? Consider how regular advertising such as print, radio and TV work. They use what is called a shotgun approach, i.e., advertising to just about everyone. Take for example radio commercials for pain relievers. Since just about anybody listens to radio, it is possible that the radio commercial only reaches a small number of people who may benefit from such medicines while most of the listeners don't have pain issues. With traditional or regular advertising, chances are high that you'll be wasting much of your money if the medium has only a low percentage of its audience interested in your product or service.

With Facebook, however, that isn't the case. Advertising on the social media giant you have a great degree of control in making your advertisements reach only the people you'd like to be reached by it. In other words, you can choose to direct your advertisements to only the people that matter – those who may be interested.

Consider for example a bike shop in the Philippines. Consider too that this bike shop specializes in fixed gear bikes or fixies. With Facebook advertising, you can filter the people who'll be reached by the owner's paid Facebook advertisement to those who are interested in bicycles, particularly fixies and only to those who live in the Philippines. But if you look at it, the Philippines is too large an area. If that bike shop is located in Metro Manila, the ad can be customized to target bikers in Metro Manila. But since Metro Manila is still large, it can be further segmented into those bikers who live in Caloocan City.

Another good example is a freelance English teacher. He or she can place an ad on Facebook promoting his or her services to Koreans who live in Seoul, are working professionals who want to advance their careers by learning English and are between 30 to 40 years old. That tutor can also specify if male or female students are preferred.

As you can see, Facebook advertising can provide a great way to really go after your very specific target demographic, which isn't remotely possible with traditional or regular advertising.

Practicality

With traditional media, it may be quite challenging to manage your advertising costs, especially if you want as much of your target market to be reached by your ads. It's because of the fact that such forms of advertising utilize a shotgun approach, which I mentioned earlier. Therefore, if you want to reach more of your target market, you'll have to reach more people in general. And advertising mediums that allow you to reach lots and lots of people are generally pricey and cost an arm and a leg.

But that's not the case with Facebook paid advertising. You can – with ease – control your advertising budget during your Facebook advertising campaigns. How? Facebook advertising gives you the opportunity to control the following aspects of your advertising cost:

- Total amount you're willing to spend on the whole Facebook advertising campaign;

- How long will your advertising campaign run for; and

- How much of your total allotted budget will be spent daily.

Suppose you only have a budget of $30 for your Facebook advertising campaign. You can set your limit at $30 and your campaign duration to let's say 10 days. Given that, Facebook will automatically limit your advertising cost to just $3 daily for the duration of your advertising campaign. Talk about budgeting, eh?

PROMOTING YOUR PRODUCTS AND SERVICES ON FACEBOOK

To make full use of the key features Facebook offers, you'll need to understand a couple of Facebook marketing best practices, which aren't necessarily unbreakable rules but merely practices to help you greatly improve your business or brand's ability to engage your customers – potential and actual – well on Facebook.

Speaking of engaging your customers, what does it really mean to do so? Engaging your customers simply mean connecting with them enough that they participate in your business or brand promotion by liking, sharing or commenting on your business' or brand's Facebook posts. The objective of engaging them is to give them a sense of participation or ownership in the business or brand.

How do engaging Facebook posts and ads look like? If you take careful notice of the Facebook pages of some of the world's top brands, a very obvious characteristic of such pages is that they don't preach or sell directly. What they do instead is connect with their audiences.

Also, people seem to be better nourished these days, i.e., they're more intelligent now than before! What this implies is that they can easily see through – or smell – any subtle attempts to make them part with their hard-earned money. They can also very easily smell your sincerity and concern for them. In this regard, it'll be good for you to keep in mind that Facebook is a social networking site first and not a multi-level marketing or classified ads website.

In their best-selling Facebook advertising book, The Ultimate Guide to Facebook Advertising, which is a great resource on the subject, authors Perry Marshall and Thomas Meloche wrote about just how different Facebook marketing is compared to traditional or regular ones by using a front porch story example:

> *Imagine a town square and you live in that area. Imagine further that your house features a front porch where you enjoy watching people pass and cultivate many beautiful plants. There*

days when you're enjoying watching people pass by and drinking from a pitcher of cold lemonade that some of those people notice your front porch's beautiful plants and approach you to ask how you keep them looking beautiful.

You offer them seats on your porch and give them glasses of cold lemonade while explaining the general principles for keeping your plants beautiful and healthy. Some of those people become so interested in plant cultivation because of your sharing that they'd be willing to spend money just to have a day with you and learn the finer details of how you grow and keep plants beautiful. You take them up on their offer and spend the next day teaching them how you do it.

In the example, were there any attempts – explicit, direct or otherwise – to sell something on the porch or promote a training program on how to grow beautiful plants on the porch? You got it right – there wasn't any! To summarize, that's how Facebook marketing is done. Selling or marketing – if any – is done indirectly and within the context of personal connections and relationships.

Always keep this in mind: Facebook marketing is all about engaging your prospects and customers. One of the best ways to do so is by giving them practical links to resources and tips on things that concern them. Another is doing your best to post content that they'll like enough to repost or share! You'll be able to engage them only by developing a relationship and to do that, you'll need to focus your posts or content on their interests and needs. And as with the porch example earlier, sales are just a result and not the immediate goal.

Another excellent way to keep your customers and prospects engaged is through posting quality and unique content as frequently as possible – daily perhaps. While it can indeed be quite tedious and cumbersome to post such content on a daily basis, especially when you're up to your neck with work, anything less frequent can increase the risk that your target audience may start to miss more and more of your great content over time due to competition from other Facebook pages that are also vying for their time and attention. The more of your posts they fail to read, the more your brand or business will slip away from their consciousness and eventually, pop goes the prospect.

A couple of studies place the optimal daily posting frequency for maximum engagement to 3 or 5 posts. But this is just based on average and your situation may very well be different and so the best approach is to experiment on what frequency works best for your business or brand.

Finally, don't forget to keep your posts interesting and fun. Keep in mind that a large part of engaging your prospects and customers successfully is having a good time. As such, always keep your posts light, interesting, helpful and to the extent possible – funny.

HOW CAN YOU MARKET ON FACEBOOK?

There are 3 tools that you can use to promote your business or brand on Facebook. These are pages, ads and groups. While each of these have their reasons for marketing existence, it doesn't mean they can't work together for the greater good, which is your profits.

Pages

These are pretty much like your personal Facebook profile page. However, these are different from yours in such a way that these are created for public figures, organizations and businesses. By simply "liking" your business' or brand's page, people can automatically receive any updates you make on those pages.

Compared to Facebook profiles that may – according to the profile owner's preference – require some level of mutual relationship among friends in order to receive regular updates, "liking" doesn't. A person can readily receive regular updates about your business or brand without having to approve any requests by liking your business or brand's Facebook page, even without your having to approve it.

Pages have the advantage of cost and ease in terms of setting up, i.e., they're free and easy to create. The disadvantage however, is that it may take a long while to develop enough foothold and fan base using pages.

We will look at this in detail in a future chapter of this very book.

Ads

The platform for advertising or promoting your business or brand on Facebook is a fantastic one. With it, you can make ads that are very much targeted at particular demographics like area, education, age and even medium used to access Facebook. The main advantage of paid Facebook ads is its ability to access particular marketing segments compared to pages. The tradeoff? They can be quite expensive, especially if you don't exercise good control or management over them.

Groups

Similar to forums for discussions, Facebook's groups have extra features not available to pages and profiles. Through it, you can create your own groups that are highly relevant to your business or brand as a way of reaching out to and engaging prospects.

The pros of Facebook groups are that they're free and can result in high engagement levels. However, managing Facebook groups can be very demanding on your time.

CHAPTER 2
MARKETING WITH PAGES

The simplest and easiest way to start with Facebook marketing is by using pages. They're basically free and doesn't require a PhD in information technology – ok, not even a degree – to set up a basic one. Plus, pages are amazingly flexible when it comes to customizing. There aren't many risks to it either.

However, many businesses still aren't able to maximize their use of their businesses or brands' Facebook pages. In fact, some even use them wrongly. But you don't want to be one of them unfortunate fellows now, do you? I thought so. As such, here are a couple of helpful tips to help you avoid their unfortunate mistakes and maximize your Facebook marketing using pages.

COVER IMAGE AND PROFILE PIC

For your business or brand's profile pic, it's a no-brainer – your logo should be your profile pic. That's it! It's a different thing altogether when it comes to choosing your cover image.

What you want to put for your cover image is entirely up to you. Some business owners use some artsy dandy artwork together with their contact details while others use pictures of their employees and/or customers. The only rule of thumb – okay, more of a nice guideline perhaps – is that your cover image must make your page look good and attract the attention of prospects and visitors.

ABOUT

Your page's "about" section is visibly situated just below your profile pic or the logo of your business or brand. As the name suggests, it's your opportunity to your page's visitors and prospects what your brand or business is all about. As such, make sure the information you'll put there is good.

So what types of information can be considered good? These include your business or brand's unique selling proposition, what product or service your business or brand provides, what it's about and other fascinating details you feel can help engage prospects and visitors more. Whenever possible, make time for writing the content of your "about" section with your Facebook audience specifically in mind. But if you're in quite a bind and happen to have a website or blog for your brand or business, consider copying the text in the "about" section of your website or blog. Also, don't neglect filling up the data under your "basic info" section too.

Oh, I forgot to mention. It's best if you keep your "about" section rather informal and friendly. Because Facebook is primarily a social network and not a business one, casual tones normally are the best when writing this section.

TABS

These refer to the small squares that are situated at the right side of the "about" section. You're given up to 10 application tabs to use for your business or brand's Facebook page. These tabs are also known as the "favorites" section. Among the required tabs on Facebook pages are "likes" and "photos". While you can position the "likes" tab wherever you like, your "photos" tabs are fixed at the first position.

You are limited to only 4 tabs for your top ones. As such, you'll have to choose which tabs to include in your top ones very wisely! A good way to go about this is by going with what you think are your prospects or visitors priorities or top interests. For example, if your business is one that has an actual physical store, location may be one of your top tabs. If your business or brand is one that conducts personal financial management seminars, consider putting an "events" tab that provides information on your upcoming seminars as one of your top tabs. Again, keep in mind that Facebook – and social media in general is all about engaging people. As such, the more you're able to engage your prospects and visitors, the better the results of your Facebook marketing will be.

THE WALL

Anything – and I mean anything – which you post on the wall of your business or brand's Facebook page will appear on the news feed of all the people who "like" that page. It's the same as when you post something on your own personal Facebook profile.

Given that is the case, ensure that you only post stuff that's either useful or interesting to your followers, fans and visitors. Avoid redundant updates and posts and try to avoid clogging their newsfeeds.

Here are some interesting things you may want to consider posting on your business or brand's Facebook page:

- Links to business or industry related materials;

- Links to blogs you posted;

- Discount coupons on your products that your page followers can avail of;

- Announcements about your latest products or services; and

- Links to other useful and practical online resources for your followers and visitors.

The key here is to post interesting and useful stuff only. As to frequency, it depends on your followers and prospects but better err on the side of caution and post only a couple of times daily.

ASK AND YOU SHALL RECEIVE - ENGAGEMENT

One of the best ways to cultivate a loyal following for your brand or business is involving them in your business or brand's Facebook page. And one of the best ways to do this is by asking them questions in your updates or posts.

Why does it help much? It's because when you ask them questions, you involve them and at their own terms – not yours. This can help give them a sense of participation or ownership in your business or brand and make them feel that they matter in your business or brand.

So what should you ask? It depends on what your niche and product or service is all about. But here's a tip to help generate the best responses from your followers: ask open-ended questions. It gives them the opportunity to really speak their mind compared to asking them questions that are answerable by just a yes or no.

One way of asking open-ended questions is by asking for their opinion on a new product or service your business or brand plans to roll out. When you do that, you subtly communicate to them that you care about them enough to customize your upcoming product or service with their needs or preferences in mind. The more you get to engage your followers with intelligent and interesting questions, the higher your chances of being positioned on top of the news feed section of Facebook.

THOU SHALL NOT SPAM

If you're looking to lose your brand or business' followers and fans as fast as possible, then spamming is the way to go. And the best way to do this is by posting about nothing else but your company's promo blurbs and making sure it doesn't have any additive value for your brand or business' followers and fans. But given your goal is the opposite, I trust that you'll do the exact opposite as well.

Keep in mind that I'm not saying you shouldn't post about your company's promotional blurbs. What I'm saying is avoid going overboard if you'd like to keep your business or brand's followers – or add more of them into the fold.

DO SOME NUMBERS CRUNCHING

One of the best features of Facebook's pages is that it gives you – as an entrepreneur – some really cool numbers and figures to crunch that can help you manage your Facebook pages marketing efforts much better. For example, if you notice that there's a significant increase in your brand or business' page, consider your most recent posts to get an idea if this is a topic or a strategy that you can use to significantly increase your fan or follower base in the future. If the figures show that there has been a significant decline in the number of fans, consider if the most recent posts may have anything to do with it so you can improve on them later on.

CHAPTER 3
USING FACEBOOK FOR TARGET (PAID) ADVERTISING

Facebook's recent financial performance greatly exceeded most analysts' expectations, which made its stock price surge, earning its shareholders a very handsome profit. The reason for the financial U-turn is primarily the big jump in its revenues, particularly from advertising.

Now, is this jump in revenue a good thing or a bad one for small business owners such as yourself and what can you learn from this regarding advertising on Facebook?

If advertising revenue has grown by so much, regardless if it came from mobile or Internet, it means that more and more businesses are advertising on Facebook. Now think about this for a moment – what would make more and more entrepreneurs advertise on Facebook? That's right – successful ads! What this means is their enjoying at least a decent level of success from their Facebook ads. And guess what, this can translate into advertising success for your brand or business as well!

Now I'm not saying that a rousing and overwhelming success is imminent when you advertise on Facebook. No, there is still a risk for unsuccessful campaigns. That risk, however, may be minimized if you work together with people who are experts on advertising on this platform – they who can help you achieve your Facebook advertising goals.

The big jump in Facebook's advertising revenues don't come without a cost, particularly to small business owners like you. It appears that the growth in advertising revenue came at the expense of organic or natural advertising reach. In simpler terms, it means that many small businesses may find it harder to reach a big percentage of their target markets without paid advertising (via pages) due to increasing competition from paid advertising.

Still, it doesn't take away the fact that advertising on Facebook is still one, if not the best, way for small business owners to promote their businesses or brands. While it becomes a bit more challenging to organically, i.e., free, reach your target markets, it also means that paid advertisements are relatively successful at reaching the same. As such, it's becoming more and more sensible to get into paid Facebook advertising for your brand or business.

FACEBOOK ADVERTISEMENTS

Facebook's ability to amass so much information about the demographics of its users makes its online target-advertising program one of the best, if not the best. As mentioned in an earlier chapter, you can practically narrow down your target audience to a particular city, age, gender and sets of interests. Further, Facebook's paid advertising allows you to see just how effective – or ineffective – your campaigns are with relevant numbers that you can crunch.

You can pay for your Facebook advertisements in 2 ways: per impression and per click. With Facebook ads that charge per impression, expressed as CPM or cost per 1,000 impressions, you pay Facebook a certain amount of money for every 1,000 impressions of your ad. An impression is when your ad appears on the news feeds section of a user's page, as an ad on the right side of the same page or on the user's mobile news feed. This is ideal if you simply want to raise awareness of for your business or brand.

But if you want serious prospects, CPC or cost-per-click is the way to go. Here, you only pay for the number of clicks on your ad. So even if your ad had 1,000,000 impressions but only 3 people clicked on it, you'll only pay for the 3 clicks.

When bidding for your Facebook ads, regardless if CPM or CPC, Facebook will inform you about similar bids in order for you to know if yours is within the market average or totally out of line with the industry's. And as mentioned earlier too, Facebook gives you the benefit of limiting your total budget so you eliminate the risk of spending more than what you're willing to.

KINDS OF ADS

You can post different types of Facebook advertisements including:

- Those that direct people directly to your business or brand's Facebook page;

- Those that lead people to your brand or business' website outside of Facebook;

- Those that help promote your business or brand's event together with a link for an RSVP; and

- Ads that feature mobile app installations and app engagement.

HIDE THEM

It used to be that Facebook allows users to choose or click on "like" on any ad. These days, it also gives users the option to hide an ad. When users choose to hide ads, Facebook asks the reason for doing so. This is also a very useful piece of information, in case users close your ads. It can help you improve the quality of your future ads for higher chances of success next time.

RIGHT ON TARGET

If you recall earlier, we discussed just how powerfully Facebook ads could target specific markets, niches or demographics. Using Facebook ads, you can practically target your market according to just about anything that can be gleaned from the profiles of all Facebook users. Location can be broken down further into state, county, zip code or city, which is great for local businesses. After targeting by location, you can further break the population target down to important demographics like age, relationship status, occupation, birthdays and education, among many others.

You can also zone in your ads to people that have just finished moving. So if you're running a yoga studio, you can target and copy write your ads to target the people who just moved into the area who are yoganatics (yoga fanatics).

You can also copy write and target people based on their hobbies and passions for your Facebook ads. Let's say you're selling fixed-gear bike memorabilia, you can put "fixie" or "fixed gear bikes" in the Interests field. You can also target your Facebook ads using an email address list of the specific people.

TAILOR FIT

Another great advantage of using Facebook's highly targeted advertisements is you can create ads for each of the various demographic groups you'd like to pitch your business or brand to. The more tightly-targeted your Facebook ads are, the greater your odds of experiencing great results from your ads.

For example, your target market are NBA fans. You can create different ads each for Warriors, Cavaliers, Spurs and Raptors fans, among other NBA teams, which you'll show only to people who have placed in their "interests" fields the names of these NBA teams.

COOL STUFF ABOUT FACEBOOK ADVERTISING

Besides the ones I mentioned, there are other really cool things about Facebook advertising that you may find useful for your own advertising campaigns on the giant social media site. These include:

Numerous Options for Targeting Boosted Posts

While you can promote your posts on Facebook by simply using the "promote this post" button, you can do a better job by using the power editor feature of Facebook instead. This will give you access to more options for targeting users to promote your posts.

You can, for example, be more specific in terms of boosting your posts by targeting according to the placement you'd like Facebook to show (the right column or in the news feeds section) or by device (computer or mobile), household membership, income and race, among many others.

Most Facebook advertisers aren't aware that total targeting options total more than 600! Other targeting options that most advertisers aren't aware of include:

- Home type;

- Home value;

- Specific ages of children (for parents);

- First time automobile buyers;

- Travelling frequency; and

- Expats.

Multiple Audiences

Facebook advertisers can access a feature called "Audience Network" so that their ads will also show up on other mobile apps aside from Facebook. The key objective for this is to meet specific advertiser goals like increased engagements and app installations. Options for targeting include look-alike audiences, core audiences and custom audiences.

The Giant Is Still...Gulp...Growing

Contrary to popular belief that Facebook's membership base has achieved a plateau already and that it has already somewhat stabilized, the social media behemoth's membership base continues to exhibit meaningful growth. Consider that from June to September 2015, it's average monthly active users increased from 1.49 billion to 1.55 billion. That's a whopping increase of 65 million in just 3 months.

Faster Ad Delivery Option

While many, if not most, Facebook advertisements use standard delivery, there is an option called "accelerated delivery", which serves advertisements a.s.a.p. This feature is especially useful for businesses or brands that have ads or landing pages that convert pretty well. This option understandably comes at a premium.

Most people think there's no such feature but it does exist. You can access this in Facebook ads' advanced options settings.

It's A Global Thang

While it's true that Facebook is an American brand, majority of its users are now non-Americans with only 17 percent of active daily Facebook users residing in North America.

Continuously Evolving Algorithms

More than just working on making Facebook ads much better overall, Mark Zuckerberg et al are working on continuously improving the algorithms (system used) in its bidding process (CPC and CPM) and ultimately, your Facebook ads' reach.

REACHING YOUR TARGET MARKET WITH FACEBOOK

Facebook continues to be the best social media-marketing platform for lead and sales generation for businesses and brands. Why? It's because of the social media behemoth's ability to use data mining with its users' behaviors that helps give you the opportunity to target particular segments and niches without having to build or buy your own prospect list.

To this extent, Facebook works together with several other behemoths in the data mining industry like Acxiom, Epsilon and Datalogix in letting brands match with gathered data via stuff like credit card data, raffles, and loyalty rewards programs for shoppers and even government records. As an advertiser on Facebook, you have access to this treasure trove of marketing information through its Partner Categories.

Basically, Partner Categories (or PC for brevity) refer to an option for targeting posts – available only to United States advertisers – that can be used to help Facebook ads in sending the right message to the right people on Facebook based on the things they do outside of it. For example, you can make use of options to target your ads to people who have made financial decisions – outside of Facebook's platform – that seem to imply that they're looking for a new vehicle.

You can use Facebook ads instead of your own list – built or purchased – to specifically target prospects who have a very high chance of acting favorably on your business or brands' advertisements. How is such information gathered? Through offline and online activities of consumers. Facebook mines data on consumers' behaviors from its various external partners like the United States

Department of Motor Vehicles (DMV), US Census and registration information, among others and combines these with its own data or information about its users in order to help you, as an advertiser in its platform, to target the right people with the right message. No wonder its advertising revenue's growing by leaps and bounds!

However, it may be a bit unnerving as a consumer to know just how much data and information Facebook is able to obtain about us, particularly in North America. But if you're an entrepreneur seeking to promote your business or brand, it's like being a kid in a candy store!

OTHER USEFUL STUFF

Just when you think we've covered much about paid Facebook advertising, wait – there's more! Here are other things you can do to make improve the effectiveness of your Facebook advertisements:

- Write advertisement headlines that address your audience directly as a person. This helps your audience feel that your ads are speaking personally and directly to them.

- A little controversy won't hurt – it can even help. It can help you convince your prospect to pay attention to your ad!

- Avoid becoming everything to all your prospects. Stick to your brand or businesses unique selling proposition, i.e., what sets it apart from the rest as well as why reading your ads are worth their while.

- The copy underneath the image you'll use for your Facebook ads must make use of open loops, i.e., texts that don't completely fit in the viewable page, which will tempt readers to click on your ads in order to read the complete text.

- The copy on your ad should be the same as the one on your landing page – exactly the same. This can help you increase the chances for opt-ins (voluntary giving of email addresses) and actual sales.

- If you're featuring a person in your ads' photos, make sure they're smiling and looking directly at the camera. It's just better than pics that look away and are frowning.

- Keep your copy writes concise and clear. Utilize it to let your prospects know what to expect if they click on the ad while keeping it within Facebook's guideline of having no more than 20% text for your ad's image.

- Show 'em the money, I mean what's gonna be in it for them if they click on your ad. For example, you can include a video or picture of a coupon or a free report of what they can expect to get for clicking on the ad. To ensure higher chances of successful sales conversions, ensure that the image on the ad is the same as in the landing page.

- Since Facebook gives you the option to modify your ads' URL displays, ensure that such displays match your website as well as your brand so it can make your prospects or viewers confident in you.

Give a clear call to action by telling your prospects what exactly is it that you'd like them to do with your brand or business' Facebook ad.

CHAPTER 4
HOW TO HELP BUILD YOUR BUSINESS OR BRAND ON FACEBOOK USING YOUR PERSONAL PAGE

If you're still not using Facebook to make people aware of your business or brand, you're wasting a perfectly great opportunity to make use of the world's most powerful marketing platform. As mentioned earlier, using Facebook gives you the opportunity to tap a lot of prospects for your brand or business. Can you imagine how many prospects – in absolute terms – you can tap even if you just aim for less than 1% of the social media behemoth's total membership of more than 1 billion people? And consider the fact that an average mobile user spends 1 minute of every 5 on Facebook – that makes for a very rich sea of prospects! Wow!

While many entrepreneurs keep their personal and business or brand pages separate, it doesn't mean you can't use your personal page to help promote the latter page and build more awareness and business about and for your brand. Consider that because business' pages contribute a lot of revenue for Facebook, it can be quite challenging to get meaningful engagement without spending on ads. Remember the issue about increasing ad revenues competing for organic or natural reach? While they seem to be working for a great number of entrepreneurs, as indicated by increasing ad revenues, why not supplement your Facebook advertising campaigns with another potentially effective – and free – supplement, which is your personal page?

The good news is that your personal page can help your business or brand's page get more attention or awareness. The bad news – if you'll look at it that way, depending on your perspective, is that it may take a bit more effort and time. But I believe that the results can be worth it.

Here's how you can use your personal Facebook page to augment your business or brand's page:

PROFESSIONALISM

If you'd like to use your personal page to supplement or augment your business or brand page, make sure that it's representative of your brand or business – it should be professional. A good and simple way of doing it is to avoid posting things that you don't want your business or brand's stakeholders – suppliers, customers, employees and prospects – to see. You wouldn't want to turn off any of your stakeholders, especially your prospects and customers.

Another good and simple guideline to help keep your page professional is to avoid posting stuff that shows you drinking, partying like hell or anything that's potentially offensive or immoral. It's very easy to lose several followers, friends and prospects with a very stupid post and very hard to win them back.

CONTROL

To maximize your efforts in using your personal page to augment your business or brand's page, it's best for you to make all your posts visible to the public, i.e., everyone. Privacy isn't an option when it comes to posts because the goal is to reach as many people as possible for the sake of your brand or business.

But accessibility to your posts should only be limited to viewing them. You'll need to keep people from just posting on your timeline or tagging you in their posts on their own or other people's walls. Turn on the option that allows you to first approve any posts or tags on your page before being shown on your wall. That way, you can minimize or even mitigate the risk of any incriminating or integrity-eroding posts making it to your page.

SOCIABLE

One of the best ways to win followers – and engage them enough for the benefit of your brand or business – is by often adding people as Facebook friends and approving as many real people friend requests as possible. Marketing and building brand or business awareness is a numbers game and as such, add as much Facebook friends as you can on your page. Just ensure they're real people.

KEEP IT UN-POLITICIZED

While it's true that we are all free to support the politicians and political issues that we want to and express such support, it doesn't mean it's good for business. Since the goal is to promote your business or brand's page, it's best not to step on other people's toes by expressing political sentiments on your Facebook page that may offend people who may have a significantly different opinion from yours. If you really need to vent off, there are many other and healthier avenues for that like friends and other people who are as open-minded as you.

POSITIVITY

Believe me, no one's going to be interested with your whines and rants. Worse, it may even turn off people enough to dislike your brand or business as well. Can you imagine the overflow to their mother teams if LeBron James or Cam Newton complained about how the NBA or NFL sucks (theoretically speaking only, ok?), respectively? That's what I'm talking about.

A good but simple rule of thumb here is this: if you can't say it to your date on your first meeting, don't say it on Facebook either.

TAG WISELY

While tagging people you've been with at events in your posts may be considered as good technique and appropriate for increasing your posts' reach to other people's followers too, it's inappropriate to tag people in posts in which they have nothing to do with just for the sake of increasing your reach. That's unwise, unethical and annoying, all of which can backfire on your attempts to promote your brand or business.

PROFILE PICTURE

If your profile picture presents you half-naked or in a really skimpy swimsuit, replace it even if you look hot. More so if your profile picture features you in a very goofy and silly mode. It's just not professional (remember the first tip?).

However, I'm not saying that you should be in a 3-piece suit or in a business dress for your profile picture. Nah, just make it interestingly decent. Since you're representing your business or brand, your picture shouldn't give people the impression that your business is either silly or stiff. Go for profile pictures that's neither too business-y nor silly or goofy. It should represent both you and your brand well enough while generating enough interest to engage your friends or your brand's prospects.

LIKE OFTEN

You can make more people more aware of your posts – and consequently your brand's page – by liking other people or brands' posts. Whenever you skip over other people's posts without "like"-ing them, you'll send Facebook the signal that you're not interested in that person or brand and over time, it'll stop showing their posts on your news feeds. And when you don't see their posts, you won't be able to like them frequently enough to make them see yours, which begins a downward spiral of posts invisibility.

More than just posts, it will also help you a lot if you like as much of other people's or brand's comments on your personal posts. You can engage more people simply by acknowledging their comments via "like". By engaging them more, you increase the chances of engaging them even more and signal to Facebook's algorithms to show their posts on your news feeds regularly.

Like often to engage often.

BIRTHDAY GREETS

Another great way to engage more people is by greeting them on Facebook on their birthdays. It sends the signal that they're relatively important to you. When people feel appreciated enough, they're encouraged to act more favorably towards you – and your brand.

POSTOGRAPHY

What I mean by this is to the extent possible, always include a photo in all your posts and don't just post using texts alone. Remember the saying that a picture paints a thousand words? As such, posts with pics tend to grab more attention from viewers and Facebook itself tends to promote posts with pictures much more than text-only ones.

And speaking of postography, always share your Instagram posts on Facebook by clicking on the "share to Facebook" button. It doubles your photographic posts exposure via dual platforms as well as increases your posts promotion by Facebook since Facebook tends to promote Instagram-shared posts more than direct photographic posts.

THE VALUE OF TIMING

The faster your posts accumulate likes and comments, the more Facebook promotes your posts. And the ability of accumulating such likes and comments quickly is highly influenced by the timing of your posts.

There are times of the day – or night – where in most of your followers tend to be actively online and it can be very beneficial for you if you're able to estimate such times. Unfortunately, the only way to really know is by trial and error – observe the relationships between your posts' timing and the number of likes or comments they get to get a rough estimate.

INFORMATIVELY INTERESTING

When it comes to engaging posts, content rules! A purely text post that says "It's freezing outside" will get way less views and engagement as compared to a post of a picture of a popsicle with clothes and shoes outside.

Posts that directly try to sell stuff is another kind of post that's sure to garner low viewership and elicit very little to no engagement and as such, must be avoided. The best way to sell – if you really need to – on Facebook is indirectly through stories or mentions. You'll have to meticulously craft your posts so that they're interesting enough to garner views and interactions or engagement to help promote and build your brand or business' page. A very good way to do this is to make use of humor and avoid being self-focused, i.e., narcissistic. Should you feel the need to post something about yourself, make it fun so people will like you and consequently, your brand or business.

CHAPTER 5
EFFECTIVE FACEBOOK
MARKETING HABITS

Mahatma Gandhi once said that our habits become our values and ultimately, our destiny. It's no different when it comes to our Facebook – or any other online – marketing destinies. Effective habits for Facebook marketing are essential for making it work.

While these are habits – character traits – and not specific strategies or tactics, these can help you optimize the latter. And here are several habits worth cultivating for optimal Facebook marketing success.

STRATEGIC THINKING

The most successful of Facebook marketing campaigns – regardless if paid advertisements or free posts – tend to go beyond the current promotions or ads. They tend to incorporate a long-term perspective of promoting their businesses or brands instead. What this means is instead of looking at how to make each and every post or advertisement excellent on a stand-alone basis, you should also look at them in terms of how they'll add up to the brand or business as a whole – a synergistic approach if you will.

So if you find that you're not thinking strategically as of now, start doing so. Brainstorm, research and at the end of the day, define clearly the direction you want to take your business or brand to and ensure that each and every post or ad on Facebook moving forward isn't just excellently engaging but also consistent with that direction.

KEEPING HEADS ON

Life isn't perfect – and so is your business or brand. As such, there will always be people who'll express a less than favorable opinion about your brand or business on Facebook. That's the way it is.

Learn the habit of not losing your head in situations like that and instead, stay professional, cool and calm in responding to such comments or opinions and look for the ways you can make your brand or business better using the information gleaned from such opinions or comments.

CONTINUOUS LEARNING

Some wise people say that learning should only stop at the grave – or in the urn. Many great people and institutions downfalls began at the moment they became so proud and complacent as to stop learning new things or ways of doing things.

So develop the habit of resisting the temptation of feeling you've already arrived after you experience one successful Facebook marketing campaign after another. The world has never been more volatile as it is now and ideas – fresh, new and better ones – are created at practically the speed of light so what you may know now about successfully marketing on Facebook may be passé tomorrow. If you don't cultivate the habit of continuous learning, you run the very high risk for a very short-lived victory in Facebook marketing for your business or brand.

WRITE, WRITE AND WRITE

Marketing – be it Facebook or any other form of such – is all about being able to communicate your business or brand's message well enough to elicit your desired action from people. The world's best marketers have, in addition to utilizing videos and pictures well, know how to communicate with words. In fact, advertising in any medium is highly dependent on the ability to write clear and catchy messages – also known as copywriting.

And since Facebook marketing is mostly about written posts, with pictures and videos also being dependent on words, developing the habit of writing frequently is a good one to cultivate. It'll help you develop the ability to write great posts and advertising copies that can generate good engagement for your business or brand.

NUMBERS CRUNCHING

Given that Facebook provides relevant figures on how well your posts and advertisements do, you have the opportunity to objectively see what works and what doesn't in terms of your Facebook marketing efforts. The worst thing to do with your campaigns is to manage them blindly, relying on gut feels and subjective opinions.

As such, another good habit to cultivate for increasing your chances of successfully marketing your brand or business on Facebook is to analyze available data. Remember, numbers don't lie – only people do.

SPECIALIZATION

Facebook marketing, as with any other form of digital marketing, is a relatively complex or multi-faceted activity. As such, it may be quite challenging to keep track of everything or to do them all well.

Given that, specialization is a good habit to cultivate as well. With the ease at which you can outsource aspects of Facebook marketing online, you can focus on your strengths and enjoy the benefit of other people's.

DETAILS DO MATTER

The best and most successful marketers have the habit of being sticklers for details because as the saying goes, the devil is in the details. It's important to pay attention to details because they can spell the difference between a Facebook marketing campaign's success and failure. Important details include the demographics of your target audience, their particular likes and interests, time of day when the ads are run or posts are made and how many people were engaged, among others.

ACT ONE TO BE ONE

If you want to be successful Facebook marketer, it's important to act like one. Cultivating these habits can help you act like a successful Facebook marketer, which significantly raises your odds of becoming one. Just keep in mind that more than the habits, consistency is just as crucial. So be consistent!

CHAPTER 6
FACEBOOK MARKETING PITFALLS TO AVOID

More than just doing the "right" things for Facebook marketing success, it's also important to avoid making crucial mistakes that can sabotage your efforts. Sometimes, a single and seemingly honest mistake is all it takes to render all the right things that you did worthless and make your Facebook marketing campaigns come crashing down to Earth. In our final chapter, we'll take a look at some of those crucial mistakes you need to watch out for and avoid for Facebook marketing success.

BEING ABSORBED BY THE BUSYNESS

As mentioned earlier, Facebook marketing is a relatively complex activity that involves several different activities. One of the risks of such is getting stuck in activities that take up so much of your time but account for a smaller portion of results. These activities include among others constantly modifying your personal and brand or business' page and being too obsessed with data that you review and analyze them almost every hour.

While such things are truly important to your Facebook marketing success, overdoing it can be counterproductive. You'll need to exercise moderation and balance so that you can also allot enough meaningful time to other important aspects of your campaign. You may be able to interpret and analyze the data well but if you don't spend enough time writing great advertising copies or posts on Facebook, you won't be able to act on whatever important insights you can glean from data analysis.

GOING AFTER THE LATEST CRAZE

With the rapid advances in technology these days, don't be surprised to find that new and "better" tools and strategies coming out every 6 months or so. Expect that hot new thing that's the craze today to be passé by that time.

Even if such new and popular releases can be very useful, it doesn't necessarily mean it's best for your campaigns. Simply adapting the latest and trendy developments for the sake of being "current" or "relevant" isn't the point. It's all about whether or not adapting such can be significantly beneficial for your brand or business' Facebook marketing campaign or not. If adapting the latest strategies or technologies will help your campaign much more successful, go ahead and do so. But if not, don't.

GUNG HO CONTENT AND PROMOTIONS

One of the worst – and common – mistakes many Facebook marketers make is not giving their Facebook posts and promotions much thought, if any at all. Many campaigns have been ruined because they post and promos were simply based on what they felt like posting and promoting or on what's currently trendy at the time.

The best way to populate your business or brand's page or ads with great content is to consider your overall promotion – bigger picture thinking and being strategic. Your content must be able to give your audience value and address their concerns and questions in ways that make them want to get in on your planned or current promotions.

If for example you're a tax consultant. The month before tax season begins, your brand's page must feature content – through posts or ads – that features or points to your page's helpful tax-related tips and advice. By the end of the month, you can announce – either via posts or paid ads – that you're available to help them out with their tax-related needs, just in time for the tax season. Your content in the month leading up to tax season points your audience to your services.

CHASING THE WIND

One of the worst mistakes that can prove to be costly for you in terms of resources and time is going after the wrong crowd. For example, if you were selling fixed gear bikes, it wouldn't make sense to go after mountain bikers or road bikers, eh? But you can innocently make that mistake by being active in biking forums that have generally more non-fixed gear bikers and promoting your business page there. You can also make the same mistake by simply indicating "bikes" in the interests' portion of your Facebook ads. It's too general and you run the risk of having your ads shown mostly to bikers who aren't even aware that fixed-gear bikes actually exist.

The best way to avoid this mistake is by paying close attention to details, particularly demographics and their interests, and not going after the latest and hottest trends for the sake of relevance. The more you know your audience, the better focused your campaigns will be and the higher your chances for succeeding in your Facebook marketing campaigns.

CHAPTER 7
WHY FACEBOOK?

Facebook marketing is a whole new world. It is one that helps you grow your business and avail multiple benefits. In this chapter, we will look at why you should take up Facebook marketing seriously and what truly sets it apart from the rest.

Reach

The first and foremost advantage of using Facebook is its sheer reach. As you know, Facebook helps you reach over a billion users all over the world who use it to login on a daily basis. This reach can help your company avail a global reach and you can successfully place your brand and products on the laps of people located all over the world. It is estimated that this number will grow in tremendous value and Facebook will reach a point where almost every single person on Earth will be connected to it. This means that the entire globe can turn into your audience base.

Potential

The benefits of using Facebook for marketing are not limited to its worldwide reach alone. It is its potential in getting noticed by all the right people in the world that makes it a great advertising tool to use. Imagine your ad getting noticed by an influential person capable of catapulting your business to reach new heights. That is exactly what Facebook is capable of doing. By choosing to place ads on it, you provide your company the chance to get noticed by hundreds of local and international influencers.

Ease of use

Facebook is extremely easy to use and has a user interface that is much appreciated for being user friendly. You can easily get started with it and start creating your pages. If you are already a Facebook user then you will know exactly how easy it is to both get started with it and keep up with it. You will have to spend no more than a couple of minutes filling in the details and you will be ready to roll. It is also just as easy to create multiple Facebook pages which can all be linked together.

Flexibility

Facebook provides you with a lot of flexibility. You can change up the setting easily and don't have to stick with the standard. You can pass the baton to someone else after the initial set up in order to take care of the rest. This flexibility is what makes Facebook one of the most preferred social networking sites in terms of marketing. Facebook also provides the user the opportunity to edit/ delete/ modify etc. which can be taken up at any point in time. If you are one of those that like to keep fixing things then Facebook will prove to be the best social networking platform for you to use.

Customization

You can customize your Facebook pages however you like. Customizing allows you to be unique and successfully send across your desired message. Customizing mostly involves choosing specific themes, pictures etc. all of which will resonate with your personal style and choice. You can hire a creative team who can customize it for you. You can draw inspiration from others as well and create something that is based off of it. In fact, the option of customization is a plus point to all those that like to set themselves apart from the rest.

Competition

With Facebook, you have the chance to keep track of your competition. This means that you can look at what your competitors are up to and what they are posting on their page. This will help you remain abreast with all the latest trends as well. You can then modify your campaign to challenge theirs and attract your audience's attention. If you have your competitors following you and vice versa, then all of you can keep each other motivated and give it your best. You can do better each time and influence your brand's popularity in a positive manner.

Facebook pages

Facebook pages are a big boon to all companies both big and small. It helps you create a unique space for your company and you don't have to bungle it in with your personal profile. You can use it to speak with your customers, inform them about any new products or offers, give them a glimpse of what is to come etc. All of this will help you generate higher sales and thereby higher profits. Facebook pages are, in fact, a great way for you to increase your overall reach and find customers by the thousands.

Costs

Advertising on Facebook can help you save on a lot of marketing costs. You don't have to set up a separate budget for it and can work with just a small amount. You can decide on a budget after you look at the response your Facebook page is receiving. If you think it is doing well then you can leave it at that but if you think it can use a little more attention, then you can consider paid ads. That will cost you a little more but will be well worth it.

Ads

Facebook ads are great for all those that have a popular page. You can make use of the situation and capitalize upon it. You can use the ads to further enhance your popularity and reach a greater audience. These ads will help relay your message and tell others about your company. You can also make use of AdSense and adwords to improve your company's income. We will look at this aspect in detail in a future chapter of this book.

Linking

It is easy for you to link your Facebook account to your website, other media sites etc. You can link your Facebook to any other platform that you like. You can incorporate the "like" button on your website, which will allow you to get as many people to visit your page.

These are just some of the many things that make Facebook great for you. As and when you start using it, you will get acquainted with its other real uses.

CHAPTER 8
ADSENSE AND ADWORDS

AdSense and adwords are both extremely useful software that you can link with your Facebook in order to capitalize on its popularity.

Those that are aware of affiliate marketing will know how the system works. You are required to have tie ups with other companies and sprinkle links to their pages all over your blog or website. Doing so will help you promote their company and in the process earn you a compensation for it.

Although affiliate marketing is a great way to capitalize on the popularity of your blog or website, it is not as easy to find the right company or companies to tie up with. Many people find it to be quite laborious to go through the whole process and end up not pursuing it at all owing to the difficulties involved in engaging with affiliate marketing.

But don't worry. Times have changed and it is not as difficult anymore to engage in affiliate marketing. In fact, it is easier than you think it is and you don't have to do anything towards getting started with it. It will only take a little effort from your end and you will be all set up to indulge in affiliate marketing.

To start with, you have to set up an AdSense and adwords account. Both of these are software owned and operated by Google. They are your one stop shop for all your affiliate marketing needs and you don't have to look any further than them.

Both AdSense and adwords are easy to work with and you will have the advantage of being associated with Google. AdSense is unique software that automatically plays an ad when somebody visits your page. The ad will appear on the right hand side of your page and can be a video or a series of images. Google is very smart and will refer to the particular person's cookies to pick an appropriate ad for them. The ad will be a result of what the person would have searched in the past and what he or she will mostly be interested in looking at. This means that there will be high chances for the person to click on the ad, thereby rendering the campaign a success.

You can choose from many options when it comes to placing your ad on the page. You can choose the size of the box, the placement, above the fold, below the fold etc. You can look at whatever works best for you and decide upon the same.

Every time successfully clicks on the ad; Google makes money off of it. It will also pay you a part of the profit that it makes. This will work in a loop where they will make money from the affiliates and pay you for hosting them.

Adwords on the other hand, works by picking and playing ads based on what words people have typed in. say for example they typed in "green purse". Adwords will suggest links to green purses by picking them out randomly and playing them as ads. As mentioned earlier, the technology is quite smart and will know what to pick and play on the site. Both AdSense and adwords can be tied up to the same page.

Once the person clicks on the ad, he or she is directed to the website of the affiliate firm. There, if they buy something, a part of the sales proceeds will be paid to Google who will in turn pay you.

Sometimes, depending on your popularity, you might be able to earn from it just by your customer visiting the page. They will not have to click on anything to buy it and just the visit will help you earn from the transaction.

Many businesses now consider this form of affiliate marketing to be one of their biggest money ringers. A company can potentially earn thousands of dollars a month just by associating with AdSense and adwords.

But there are a few rules to bear in mind when it comes to both. For starters, you should avoid clicking on the ads yourself as that will not go down too well with Google. They will track your IP address and know that you are clicking on the ads yourself. If Google finds out that a lot of the clicks are coming from you then it can disassociate with you without prior warning. If you think it is going a bit too slow for you then you can request people to click on the ads if you like but it should all come from unique IP addresses and not the same place.

You have to reach a minimum amount before being able to encash it. The minimum amount is $100, which Google will pay into your account after the 15th of each month. You can request for a delay in payment if you like.

You have to seriously consider tying up with Google adwords and AdSense if you wish to capitalize on your Facebook page's popularity. Your company can start earning a parallel income which will supplement your regular income.

CHAPTER 9
FAQs ABOUT FACEBOOK MARKETING

Here are some frequently asked questions about Facebook marketing that you need to look into to drive away any doubts on the topic.

Is it important to use media?

Yes. It is extremely important for you to make use of media to add to your Facebook campaigns. Be it a picture or a video, you have to append it to your Facebook campaign as it will garner a better response. People will be drawn more to these than they would be to just a few fancy words even if it is written in a unique and catchy font. You have to supplement almost all your campaigns with a picture or a video if possible. They should be relevant to the text that it accompanies.

Is it necessary to be part of Facebook groups?

Ideally yes. By being a part of a Facebook group, you will be able to reach out to a large number of people. This can help you increase your overall value as people will take a liking to your active participation. Facebook groups are meant to help you not just connect with other like-minded people but also potential customers. You can take part in these groups and suggest that they like your page or your products. You can consider it a form of subtle advertising.

Is it possible for b2b companies to use Facebook for promotions?
This is one question that gets asked most often. Many people wonder if it is possible for business oriented companies that cater to other businesses to promote themselves on Facebook. The answer is yes. You can make use of Facebook to promote your business, which caters to other businesses. You can successfully advertise your products and services, which they can take a note of. We will look at this topic in detail in a later chapter of this book.

Is it better for me to sell on Facebook than my website?
Yes. That is a good idea as you will have a lot more people visiting your Facebook site than your website. However, you must not replace the latter with the former and can sell at both these sites. You can redirect people to your website once they visit your Facebook page by expressly telling them to do so. The landing page should be clear and free

from unwanted clutter. You can take orders on your Facebook page as well if you think that will work well for you.

Is there a way to increase the like count?

There are many ways to increase the likes count on your page. First, you can send requests to all the people on your profile and request all of them to send it to people on theirs. You must also incorporate the "like" button on your website and other places where people can access it. The like count is not affected by other pages that like you and takes into consideration only the individual likes. You can track the likes if you wish to and have a particular number in mind to make it easier for yourself.

Where can I find people to help me with content?

There are many places where you can find people who can help you with creating the unique content. If you want something permanent in nature then consider hiring a team for it. We will look at some of the requisites to hire a social media management team in a later chapter of this book. But if you want a quick solution then you can consider looking for people to hire on a freelance basis. These can be found at places such as fiverr and freelancer where you can post a job for people to notice and apply.

How often should I post on my page?

There is no one number that can be considered the gold standard. You should come up with a number based on your experience and what you think has worked best for you. The number can be 3, 4 or even 5 posts a day depending on how much information needs to be relayed to your audience. The basic idea is to maintain the right amount and not overload your audience with too much information. You shouldn't bewilder them by giving them too much or bore them with too less. It should be just right and enough to keep them glued. You must also consider appropriate times to update the posts. They should follow a set frequency.

How often should I be replying?
This question needs to be answered in the same breath as the previous one. You have to find a strategy that works best for you. Although it is ideal for you to reply to your customers as often as you can, it might not really be practical to do so. Therefore, the best is to pick out the few that are your loyal customers and who bring in most business. Reply to them as much as you can to remain in their good books. If there is a common theme in many of the queries then take of that as well by replying with an answer that can apply to all.

Is better to campaign for the current audience or future ones?

That depends on how many customers you currently have on your page. If you have a large enough customer-base then you can consider catering to them alone. You don't have to put in efforts to find new ones. On the other hand, if you have only a few customers and need more, then you can consider targeting new ones in order to increase the number of customers that you have and then create campaigns. But remember that it needs to be either or as doing both might cost you a lot more than what you can financially handle.

How can I get my customers to help out?

There are many ways in which you can get your customers to promote your brand and products. You can start by announcing contests and encouraging them to contribute to it. Secondly, you can announce prizes for anyone who manages to share your page the most and bring in newer customers, which is better known as referral rewards. You can also tag these fans to posts in order to make them feel appreciated and valued.

Can I link my different media?

Yes you can. You can link your different media together in order to maintain uniformity. You can make use of the

Facebook to twitter app to connect the two platforms together. It will pay to unify the two audiences and increase your universal visibility.

These form the different FAQ's that get asked on the topic that will help you understand the topic better.

CHAPTER 10
FACEBOOK OFFERS ONLY

There are a few Facebook only offers that you can take up in order to appeal to your audience. Here they are in detail.

After sales

You can offer exclusive after sales services on your Facebook page. This means that people can reach out to you on your Facebook page when they wish to have a query answered or seek information on something. You can mention the same on the bag that you give away with your product. You must also explicitly tell them that you can be reached on your Facebook page in case they have a doubt over something. You must then provide them with a separate section on the page where they can voice their question or call up the customer care by looking up the number provided there.

Feedback forum

You can utilize your Facebook page as a feedback forum. Encourage people to speak up and tell you what they think about your brand and products. Give them an outlet to voice their honest opinion and don't unnecessarily bash their opinion. They should be able to speak their mind out and you must be patient in lending them an ear. Once they are done, you must make the effort of answering them. Again, provide them with practical solutions instead of simply acknowledging their queries.

Exclusives

Another great idea is to offer exclusives to your Facebook customers. These exclusives should be available online only and not anywhere else including your stores. When people walk into your store, you should tell them that you are offering to them an exclusive design that they can only buy online. You can have a handy image of the product to show them and explain its unique features. If you want to make it a simple campaign, then consider simply changing the color of an existing product. But if you want to make it a bit more appealing then come up with an entirely new product that they can only buy online and not anywhere else.

Discounts

Giving away exclusive online discounts is a great way of attracting people to your Facebook page. You can give them a 10, 15 or 20% discount coupons, which they can redeem while checking out at the online store. This offer should not be present anywhere else and must be a Facebook exclusive. The discount needs to be substantial enough for your customers to take notice and decide to buy from your Facebook page. If someone walks into your store or if you have people visiting your online website then you can add in a disclaimer instructing them to avail the discount online.

Competitions

Hosting competitions online never fails. You can come up with contests which will help your customers participate and enjoy themselves. The contests can be anything that you think will interest your audience. Don't stick with run off the mill contests like coming up with slogans and introduce something unique like a quiz contest or a crossword. Try keeping it as interesting for them as possible and avoid making it too plain as that might not appeal to the younger generation as much. Maintain a set schedule for announcing the contests so that your audience can remain prepared for one.

Tie-ups

You can have tie ups with other brands. These tie ups should allow you to both promote your brand and the other person's as well. The tie up can involve providing a discount coupon which can be redeemed when purchasing a product from the other company. Similarly, they should also provide customers with a coupon that can be used at your store to avail a discount. Remember to tie up with those companies that have just as many customers you or more and not lower than you. The two of you should lie on the same plane when deciding to tie up.

Like

You can offer a reward to everyone that likes your page. This means that you give away something every time somebody likes your Facebook page. This can keep it interesting enough for people to make the effort of liking the page for you. You can send them mails informing about the same. The price you offer needs to be substantial enough though and not something that will make them change their mind. Have a set target in mind in terms of the likes that you would like to attract within a month.

Events

You can organize events where all your Facebook customers can meet. Organizing such an event will not only allow you to get everybody under one roof but also increase your customer base. You should ask them to bring along a friend or two, who can like your page as well. Organize the event in such a way that the focus remains on your customers. You should make them feel wanted and appreciated. Tell them what the event is being organized and how their feedback will be valued. You must also ask them for some valuable suggestions that they can impart for you to do better.

These form the different Facebook exclusives that you can indulge your customers in to increase your page hits.

Topics to discuss at events

When you decide to organize the events for your customers you will have to decide on the topics that will be discussed. Here are some.

As your audience what they think about your Facebook marketing campaign. You can prepare a questionnaire for them with multiple choice questions to make it easy for them to answer.

Also ask for suggestions about how you can improve it and what they would like to see. Here, you have to let them write what they want instead of giving them choices.

Ask them about any grievances that they have and tell them you will be rectifying it.

But remember to keep it short and simple instead of boring them. Before it ends, you must ask them if they will be interested in attending more such events and how the events themselves can be improved.

CHAPTER 11
FACEBOOK MANAGEMENT TEAM TO HIRE

As mentioned earlier, it is important for you to hire a team which will help you maintain your Facebook page.

Description

The first thing is to provide your applicants with a proper job description. You should tell them exactly what the job will entail and give them as much information about it as possible. They should come in prepared for the interview and know exactly what will be required of them. The description should also entail what they should be doing or saying on Facebook for you and apply only if they are up for the task.

Past experience

The first thing to check is their past experience. Look at where they have worked and what they have done in the past. They should have had sufficient work experience in the field of media management. They should bring in experience that will benefit your firm and make your brand more visible to the public. If they have not handled tasks like that in the past then look at what they have done and whether it is relevant to what you expect of them.

Personal popularity

Although this is not really important, you can consider looking into their personal popularity to see if they can significantly contribute to your brand. Go through their social media profiles to see if they are popular enough and have a good following. Their personal popularity can help your company in a big way in that you can get noticed by everybody in their list. But that should not really be a criterion for you to consider while looking for prospective people to manage your Facebook account. Even if they are not too popular, they might be able to pull in a large enough crowd.

Tech savvy

This goes without saying. People that you hire to take care of your Facebook account should be tech savvy. They must possess sufficient knowledge on how to operate the Facebook account and keep it updated. They should know to work with the latest technology and use it to help your company. If someone does not know how to do operate things then they might delay your progress. If you think someone is good enough but lacks the right knowledge then you can consider training them first before hiring them.

Competitive nature

The people that you hire need to be competitive. They should maintain a competitive nature and feel the need to outdo the competition. They should be instructed to keep an eye on what others are up to and keep up with them. Look at their past experience to see if they have been competitive at their previous work. They should be ready to take any challenge head on. This aspect is especially necessary when it comes to Facebook marketing as it can get pretty competitive out there and you must be ready to accept and excel at a challenge that is thrown your way. You should tell your team about the same in order to prepare them in advance.

Creativity

The level of creativity should be above average when you wish to hire people to manage your Facebook page. They should be able to come up with campaigns that will keep people interested and up their level of enthusiasm. The campaigns should be aimed at everyone and not just a particular set of people. Although creativity is subjective, you should look at what the candidates have done in the past to ensure that they are the right fit for your company.

You should give them the freedom to do what they want and not have to barge in every time to correct them.

Enthusiasm

The team that you hire should be enthusiastic. They should not showcase only initial enthusiasm and then allow it to fizzle. They should keep the mood going and look at every campaign enthusiastically. You should also keep their spirits high by telling them how good they are and how they should keep up the good work. You can consider announcing a price every month which will be awarded to the most enthusiastic media manager. You have to specify the guidelines that will be taken into consideration while choosing the best.

Eye for detail

The team members should have an eye for detail when it comes to managing your social media campaign. They should know what will appeal to the audience and work towards incorporating all the tiny elements. Having an eye for detail can also involve knowing what needs to be added in to the existing content in order to make it a little more likeable by the entire populace. For example, if it is a beauty cream that is being campaigned for, then highlighting a small detail such as the absence of a chemical in it can make a big difference.

Teamwork

Team work is of extreme importance when it comes to managing a Facebook page. You should hire people that will get along well. Of course you won't have this at the back of your mind when you are hiring the right candidates to work for you but, it is a must that you look at their past experience to see if there were any issues there that should concern you. You must ask them about the same to clear the air on it.

Defined goals

It is important to give your team defined goals that will help them know what to and what not to do. The goals should pertain to the marketing campaign and what they should be doing for your brand and products. The predefined goals should include knowing how the campaign will look, the pictures to be used, the choice of words etc. These defined goals need to be discussed before the start of every campaign to ensure that the team and you lie on the same page.

Training

It will be necessary for you to provide your team with training from time to time. You should teach them about new technologies and how they can make use of trending topics to garner attention. The training should happen every few days in order to create a team that will know exactly how to influence an audience.

These form the different aspects to consider while hiring a team to manage your Facebook page.

CHAPTER 12
FACEBOOK STRATEGIES FOR B2B

Here are some strategies that b2b businesses can employ to generate an interest amongst target businesses.

Target the right companies

This is obvious but what needs to be kept in mind every single time you host a campaign. You should bear in mind the target audience and generate a campaign that will specifically appeal to them. The target audience in question here is the companies that you will be targeting your products towards. The companies to target should all be sent a like request so that they remain aware of your online presence. Next, you should look at the companies that are on your list and create campaigns specific to them. See what they have liked in the past and give them something similar. For example, if you create plastic boxes and supply it to restaurants, then look at what they currently use or have liked and design something similar but better so that they will easily move to you.

Go beyond

It is important for you to reach beyond the companies that you have on your Facebook or on your Facebook page. You should target companies that are present on other media such as twitter and Google+. You should create campaigns that will appeal to all the companies and not just a few in particular. For that, you have to think of schemes that will apply universally. For example, if you deal in supplying party equipment, then look at the gamut of your clients and see what they all have in common which can be tapped into. Once you find it, you can design the campaign around it and lace links to your Facebook page on twitter, Google+ etc.

Categories

You have to divide the people into different categories to make it easy for you to target the campaigns. As you know, Facebook provides you with the option of dividing all your different clients into separate categories based on a common link. You will also find it easy to find these companies just by looking at the name of the category. For example, you can divide some based on their name, some on location etc. Bifurcating that way will make it easier for you to work with them.

Discussions

You can encourage your clients to hold regular discussions on your page. They can speak on topics that are pertinent to everybody present on the page. You can initiate the conversations and then let them take over. Try to keep it both light and interesting. Touch on topics that will make them respond. That's a good way to keep them interested in taking part on whatever is happening on your page. But remember, you shouldn't allow it to become all about having conversations alone and must get them to focus on what you have on offer for them.

Incentives

You can announce incentive rewards to whoever brings in most likes. This is the same as individual customers brining in other customers. You can offer a reward such as a discount on their next purchase or some such thing that will keep their interest going. The point is to get them to take an interest in spreading word about you. You have to keep the incentive program going for some time and not stop it until you have reached the ideal target in terms of likes accrued.

Retarget

Don't worry if you have lost an audience owing to concentrating on a particular group. You can retarget them by creating schemes that are specific to them. Look back at what has worked with them in the past to bring in the same back. Retargeting is a great idea for all those that wish to increase or maintain their customer base. You can make a list of everybody that you wish to target and tailor make the schemes for them. Work with your team to create these specific strategies that will work towards attracting and maintaining your audience's interest.

Not too serious

But try to keep it light and not make it too serious. If you make it too serious then your targets might get bored. Just because you are advertising to other businesses does not mean you make it very boring. You have to treat them like individuals and come up with schemes that will hold their interest. Invest in the same type of colorful banners and other such eye catching material that will appeal to these businesses. But know where to draw the line as making it too casual might make the main point disappear. You should make sure the idea is clear but relayed in a fun manner.

Link it

You have to link all your different social media platforms. Be it Google+, twitter or LinkedIn, you should link all of them together in order for your clients to relate to you in a better manner. Link them and encourage everybody on these platforms to like or at least visit your Facebook page. Doing so will help you increase your like count.

These form the various b2b Facebook strategies that you can adopt to amplify your reach.

CHAPTER 13
CUSTOMER IDENTIFICATION AND 80/20 ANALYSIS

Here is a customer identification chart that will help you segregate your customers into individual categories.

70-90%

This is the main category of customers that you should design your campaigns for. They can quite easily be your repeat customers. They will most likely return to buy from you and so, must do everything in your power to appeal to and retain them. This category of customers will be well organized and know exactly what they want to buy from you. So, you have to be a little smart in your suggestions to them. You should look at what they are mostly interested in buying and suggest whatever you think they will take a liking to. Say for example one of them is looking at a pair of grey jeans to buy. You should suggest a nice top that will go with it or a belt that will compliment it. Your choice should be smart enough for them to take the suggestion seriously. You have to allow them enough time to make their choice though as bombarding them with several suggestions will work counter productively for you. Try to have a list of complimentary item suggestions handy, which you can pull out to suggest to these people. That way, you will not waste time in making the suggestions. You should also keep in touch with these people after they finish buying from you. You should call and text them regularly in order to remain in their good books. You must assist them with after sales services as well such as demonstrations and set ups. You can categorize these people to place in a separate category.

50-70%

The next category of customers is the 50-70%. In this category, you will find all those that are almost as organized as the people in the previous category but not as smart as them. You can appeal to them by creating a sense of urgency. For example, you can tell them that an offer will last just as long as the stocks last. This sense of urgency will cause them to settle for the item. But be careful, you must not force it upon them at the last minute as they will not be keen on it. You have to allow them sufficient time to make their choice. The people in this category generally prefer to go about a list that they would have prepared and pick up the items accordingly. So, here too, you should have a list ready that will mention all the complimentary goods that you can suggest to them. They will appreciate your suggestion especially if really does make sense to them. You have to keep in touch with these customers as well since they will also be your potential return customers.

30-50%

The next category is the 30-50%. People that lie here will be extremely restless. They will not wait for an offer and will be keen on buying whatever they fancy. In fact, they will instantly take a liking to something that they think looks colorful and fancy. So, the best way to appeal to these is to put on display a set of fancy items that will catch their attention. On your Facebook page, you should upload a picture of all the most colorful and fancy things that are sure to appeal to this category of people. But remember that they will be pretty restless which means that they will move from one thing to another within the blink of an eye. So, to contain them, you must keep supplying them with interesting stuff which will hold their attention. They will add in the items into their bag only if they find it just as they are checking out. To convert them into regulars, you have to keep sending them updates on new items that you have stocked in your store.

10-30%

The next category of people is the 10-30%. These people will be on the look-out for schemes that will help them carry with them something for their near and dear ones. So, they will take up an offer which will give them a duplicate of what they are buying or a scheme where they need to pay half the price for buying two things etc. Such schemes are sure to be a hit with people that belong to this category. So, you have to have schemes like these present on your page at all times if you wish to capture the fancy of this particular set of audience.

0%

The last category is the 0%. These people might not be interested in buying from you at all. It will take a lot of effort from you to retain these and get them to buy from you. You might actually be wasting your time with these and it is best for you to look past them.

Don't worry if you are unable to identify the different customers easily. It will take time and a little effort from your end to find them. The important thing here is to segregate the audience in a way that helps you aim specific campaigns at them.

The 80/20

The 80/20 analysis is one, which you can use to know what is working well for you and what is not. The analysis takes into account everything that you currently have and helps you find the best amongst the lot. Say for example, you want to know what product is working well for you. For that, you should make a list of all the products and record them one after another. Next, mention the sales numbers next to it and total everything up. You must use the cumulative tabulation method. Once done, divide each of the individual numbers with the resultant cumulative number to get the individual values. These will form your final results. Here, you will find the 20% products that are contributing to your 80% results. But don't get confused here; the 80 and 20 don't have to add up to give you 100. For example, 7 of your products might be giving you 80% results.

The basis of this theory states that 80% of your overall productivity will have a 20% factor contributing towards it. Therefore, 80% of your sales will be generated by 20%of your overall products. Your task is to find the 20% and work on bettering it.

Similarly, you can do 80/20 analysis to find the best campaign for you. You can make a list of all your campaigns on Facebook and see what has worked well for you and what has not.

CHAPTER 14
TIPS AND TRICKS THAT WORK ON FACEBOOK

Have a fixed agenda

It is important for you to work with a fixed agenda. This means that you need to set yourself reasonable goals and go after them when you wish to attain more visits and page hits. The only way to increase your visitor count is to write down your goals and set yourself time limits within which to attain them. Before you know it, you will be able to capture a larger audience base all interested in you on a permanent basis.

Likes

One simply cannot under estimate the value of likes of Facebook. These likes are after all what will help you remain popular on the website. These Facebook likes will act as your biggest promoters. You will show up first on any search result if you have a large enough "like base". You can go from being a non-existing name to a big one just by getting people to like you. You can send these like notifications to everyone in your group and also get them to share it with others in theirs. Set yourself a "likes" goal and go after it to improve your visibility and reach.

Hide content

One great way to get many people to like your page is by hiding valuable and interesting content behind it. You have to tell your audience that there will be something valuable waiting for them if they like your page. Ensure that the giveaway is substantial enough to not disappoint them as you don't want to risk causing them to change their mind about it. You have to make it as colorful and glittery as possible for them to take notice and respond to your call to action request. It should literally ask them to do whatever you want them to.

Like and share

Use the like and share buttons for different purposes. For example, use the like button to ask people whether they like what you have on offer for them and the share button if they are likely to buy it from you. Both like and share together can also be an option that your audience can choose.

Exclusives

Everybody in this world likes an exclusive and you can take advantage of this quality. By offering Facebook only offers to your customers you can capitalize upon their need for such deals. The offers can pertain to giving them something that they cannot find anywhere else. Be it a buy 1 get 1 offer or a free gift on the purchase of an item from your store. These exclusives are a great way to capture your audience's attention and keep them interested for long.

Mobiles access

Facebook is a great platform for any form of promotion no doubt but it is most effective in terms of mobile phone advertising. As you know, millions of people now use mobile phones to access Facebook and you can look to developing something that will look great on the cell phone. Work with your team to come up with something that will make it easier for your customers to look at and buy your products on a mobile phone. You can make the pages exclusive and not relevant to whatever you are using in your other campaigns. This will also make it extremely exclusive.

Stalk them

It is a good idea for you to stalk your customers. But do it silently. Hire a team to go through all their likes and dislikes. Make a recording of everything so that you can send them emails that will specifically cater to their taste. Employ a team to generate the emails for you keeping in mind the different likes and dislikes and after going through their purchase history.

Call to action

The call to action aspect of Facebook advertising is probably the most important and what you have to take up seriously. Call to action refers to asking your customers to do something for you. This can include liking your page or buying something or sharing your page etc. You have to explicitly tell your audience to do something for you if you want to promote your brand and products the right way. You should make it as obvious as possible in order for them to take definite and quick action. Don't think they will do something if you don't tell them to and it should be your priority to tell them everything explicitly.

Paid ads

The paid ads option on Facebook can help you in many different ways. Right from spreading word about your company to telling people where to find you, you can use the paid ads option to your company's advantage. One great feature of the paid ads is that you can use it to draw people's attention to your latest offerings. This can be any new products or a new promotion that you have on offer for them. The paid ads option is a convenient way for you to announce any important aspect of your company.

Remember that you don't necessarily have to have a Facebook page to create an ad. You can do so by choosing the clicks to website objective, which will help you create Facebook ads. These are great for your company as you can reach an audience without having to create a Facebook page. However, this type of ads that are not connected to a Facebook page will only appear on the right hand side of a page and not in the news feed. But that really should not matter as long as you have interesting content to offer. We did a whole segment on paid ads which you can read again if you want more details on it. Think of it as a great way for you to increase your customer base.

Sponsored stories

Those that regularly use Facebook will know that Facebook stories appear on your wall when someone comments or likes a page. You can influence this aspect and make it a bit easier for your story to be discovered. Go to your ad creator tool where on the left hand side you will find the option of sponsored stories which you have to tick in order to activate. Doing so will make you a bit more visible and your sponsored stories will appear on the walls of others that use it or access your Facebook page.

Unique headline

Facebook now offers the chance for you to change the headline of the page. This means that you need not leave the headline as is, which will be a copy of your page title and can modify it to make it unique. The headline can be something that will capture your audience's attention and want them to visit you. Come up with something unique and interesting every time and make your audience want to visit your page to look at what the offer is all about instead of simply reading the title and going back.

Explore everything

You should explore all the options that Facebook offers to its users. This can include using the ads to tell people about yourself or promoting a new aspect of your business or telling people about your company's vision and mission, drawing in the attention of advertisers etc. There are just so many things that you can do using Facebook and Facebook ads that you will not tire with it easily. The key is to make use of all the right features in all the right ways in order to attain the best results. This might take a little while but you will find the activity well worth it.

Team work

Remember that Facebook is all about teamwork and it will pay for you to allow others to help you with your advertising. This can be sharing the responsibility with your team or with a friend. You have to allow them access to your page where they can modify it any which way that they like. The key is to allow as many different opinions as possible in order to encourage the page to look as versatile as possible. You can access the option of adding in another administrator by choosing the "add new user" option.

Bidding options

You can choose from many bidding options on Facebook. You can choose from clicks, impressions and other such options. Once you do, your objectives will be automatically fulfilled. You have to set yourself a budget and go about it in an orderly fashion. If you fail to ready a set budget then you might end up spending a lot more than what you actually intend to. Draw up a financial plan and go as per it in order to control your campaigning costs.

Budget options

There are two main budget options to choose from with one being the daily option and the other one being the lifetime option. The daily option will help you set up a daily budget that you can set for yourself. Once that budget is exhausted, your ads will automatically stop playing. This is great for all those that wish to operate within a fixed budget. The other option is the lifetime budget. With this, you can choose a budget that will allow you to run the ads uninterrupted through the course of the campaign. Once the budget stops so will the ads. You have to plan the money spending accordingly.

Flexibility

The budgeting options on Facebook are quite flexible. You can easily modify and edit it after your campaign successfully starts running. You don't have to worry about not being able to change the settings up once you have everything going. You can change the end date of the campaign as also the budget that you have picked for it. This flexibility is vital for all those that like to manage a campaign as and when it begins without setting any prior goals towards it. You can save on quite a bit of money if you pick this option.

Images

You should work towards incorporating as many images in your ad campaign as possible in order to make it visually appealing to your audience. It is no secret that these images will pull in a bigger crowd and help your ad campaign take off. You have to indulge in adding pictures that are of great quality and customized to suit the needs of your readers. Try adding in pictures that drive over the message effortlessly and don't require you to add in too much information about your campaign. Take inspiration from what has worked for you in the past and build on ideas that are sure to be a hit.

Trial and error

Facebook allows you to add in up to 6 images without charging you anything extra. This can help you indulge in trial and error and try out as many different images as possible before picking the right one for your campaign. Again, look at what has worked for you in the past and adopt the same. You can also draw inspiration from another company's ad campaign and incorporate some of its successful elements into yours. Make a note of everything that has truly worked well for you.

Size matters

The overall size of the pictures and the text really matter when it comes to establishing a successful campaign. This means that you have to ensure the text does not exceed 20% of the total space that is available. The picture to text ratio should be kept in mind while designing the campaign. If everything overlaps then it will get a bit too confusing for your audience. You have to allow the images to remain prominent and add the text next to it. Don't worry if you get it wrong the first few times, you will be able to fix the issues as and when you make progress.

Image size

The size of the image to be uploaded is just as important as the ratio of image and text. You should ensure that you pick an image that is 1200x627, which is the standard option that Facebook recommends. This size picture will help you send across the right message to your audience as they will able to see clearly whatever you are trying to tell them through the images. Once you upload it, you can ask others for their opinion about the same and modify it if necessary. There is software available for free, which will help you crop the images to the ideal size. You can use them to find the right sizes for the images and also add in the text appropriately.

Word count

Pay close attention to your word count as well as it is important to keep it within limits. You don't want to bore your audience by giving them something lengthy and boring. You should limit it to 100 and 250 words and not any more. Speak with your content management team and instruct them about the same. They should be told to condense the information into something that will be a concise version and fit in well with the word count requirement.

Spacing

It is best for you to post new posts consistently all through the day and ensure that the posts all contain unique content. Try to come up with a frequency that suits your business. Some like to update every 8 hours or so but you can delay it more if you like. But you have to maintain a consistent time gap in order to remain predictable. Your audience should wait for your next post to come through.

Target audience

One big way in which people can build on their popularity is by influencing their target audience. Target audiences refer to those people to whom you are specifically catering your products and campaigns to. Doing so will help you increase your reach and popularity. You can use many different types of filters to bifurcate your target audience such as age, country of origin, education etc. Doing so will help you place your campaign in the right place and sell your products to the right audience. You can work with a team of experts who can advise you on the things that you can do to appeal to the right audience. It should go beyond mere taglines and pictures and you should incorporate many other elements that will specifically cater to the right audience. Try adding in a few trending topics that will be a hit with the younger generation. Similarly, add in elements that are specifically targeted at your target audience. Make a list of all their likes and dislikes and then go about designing your campaign.

Expansion

You have to focus on either bettering your relations with your current audience or appeal to new ones. You cannot have both as you will end up increasing your overall costs and that is not really a good option for you. You should focus on whoever is part of your current group and campaign specifically to them. Try to cater to their interests and give them material that will keep them hooked. On the other hand, if you wish to increase your audience base then you must give them new content and lure them towards you. While doing so, you might have to forgo looking into the interests of your current customers. Speak with your team and decide on which aspect you would like to pursue.

Mailing

If you are only interested in expanding your current base and do not wish to add in any new customers then you can append your mailing list to your Facebook account. Doing so will help you look at everybody that exists in your list and you can target them in particular. This is a great way to have everyone in the same place and you don't have to formulate a new list. It is ok to combine them with your

Facebook exclusive audience and can create campaigns that will successfully appeal to both.

Measure

It is quite important for you to measure everything including the number of people that you are targeting. You should avoid having too many or too little as either can cause your costs to go up. As is the case with most other aspects, you have to plan your audience out and keep a number ready. Once that number is reached, you can stop. You can make use of the meter that is provided by Facebook to keep track of the number of people and classify them based on their demographics.

Categorize

You will make it extremely easy for yourself if you categorize the different people and put them into standard categories. For example, have a category for all people who have a birthday coming in the month, one for those that have achieved something recently etc. When you classify your Facebook audience like so, you successfully divide them in such a way that helps you identify the different categories and aim your campaigns at them in particular. You can have as many categories as you like and assign a different name to each to divide them based on interests.

Facebook to store

If you need help shifting people from online store to your physical store then you can make use of campaigns that will draw them into your shop. Announce a campaign where they can pick something online and redeem it at the store. This will ensure that you have customers walking into your store to redeem the offer and you can contain them there by showcasing something appealing that is only available at the store. This strategy works well if you have a local group of people that are sure to take advantage of this offer.

Competitions

Contests and competitions will never fail you. These interest pretty much everybody and you can successfully draw in a large audience. The key is to organize something that will not only captivate their imagination but also cause them to visit your page more often. These competitions need not always pertain to your company and products alone. Try holding something that will promote your business whilst also appealing to a large audience base that will be interested in things apart from providing captions and pictures. But don't forget to get the kids involved as well as that can help you increase your popularity considerably.

Article box

Facebook gives you the option of modifying the article box and adding in a custom image and caption. As you know, Facebook automatically assigns you an article box carrying the image on the left, the headline and meta-data on the right. You can modify this and alter it to suit your campaign by inserting a custom image and message. You can make use of bitly URL for the same and customize the article box to your liking. You can make use of pics that will help you drive across the message without having to use any captions.

Insights

It's been mentioned quite a few times that you have to look back at what has already worked for you and make use of the same to help you further. But then, how can you know what has worked for you and what has not? Well, it's simple; you make use of insights to look back at your own posts to see what has gone your way and what has not. You can have a look at all the shares, likes and reposts that your original post has received, which will tell you how popular it was. You can pick out the ones that have fared well and repeat them.

Videos

You have to compulsorily append videos every now and then if you wish to garner a larger audience's attention.

These videos should contain interesting content that will appeal to your chosen crowd. Videos have the unique quality of being a bit more relatable, which makes it great for you to drive across a point easily without having to do too much for it. Just incorporate the message into a well-crafted video and you are ready to roll. Get a professional to both design and capture the video for you in order to make it appealing enough for your crowd to appreciate.

Pictures

You have to keep switching up both your display and cover pictures from time to time. This will help build and interest amongst your audiences. Both these should be a good representation of what you company is currently up to. You have to pick the best images amongst the lot and switch up your pictures every now and then.

Tagging

The importance of tagging cannot be stressed upon. You have to tag people and companies in your posts in order to increase both your visibility and your importance. Tag whoever is associated with you and mention a note about them. Doing so will help you connect better with the tagged people as well as your audience. It doesn't matter if the tagged person is in your list or not, you will have the chance to connect with newer people. Don't worry if you are making someone famous in the process. They will be thankful for it and might return the favor.

Share

It should not be limited to tagging alone. You should also share any content that your fans have created for you. This can be something that they have customized for you or created using your products. It's a great way to encourage your audience to partake in your company's activities and be a part of your campaign. In fact, make it a priority to incorporate a fan made post on a weekly basis to help them feel wanted, loved and appreciated. You will be surprised at the response that you will be able to garner from it all.

Ask and tell

One unique aspect about Facebook users is that, they like to ask questions and have them answered. They will also like to answer questions by taking surveys. Therefore, by incorporating both these aspects, you can reach out to a lot more people. Start by incorporating the option of leaving behind a question about your brand and allow your audience to voice their opinion. Next, leave behind a survey that your audience members can take in order to know their honest opinion on something.

Quiz

Quizzes can be just as interesting as contests. You can host a quiz where you ask questions pertaining to something popular like a trending song or something that will keep them glued to your posts. You can supplement it with a nice picture of something that is related to the question. The basic idea is to get people talking about whatever you have posted. Try to keep the answers to the quiz relevant to what you are offering and announce a prize for all those that answer it first.

Hashtags

You know have Facebook hashtags as well, which sounds like a twitter cross over. You can make use of hash tags to mention people and also trending topics. That way, you can remain popular on both the social media platforms. However, this feature on Facebook is not really popular or not as much as it is on twitter. But you can manage to get a few hits as people will be able to type in the hashtag name and find it successfully.

Inspiration

Draw and share an inspirational quote to attract your audiences. The inspiration can come from anywhere and must be relevant to your brand. For example, if you are a company that sells toys; draw an inspirational quote from Ruth Handler and place it on your Facebook page. It will make your audiences relate with the quote and maybe decide to buy a doll from your store. Similarly, add in quotes and other elements that will remind people about something that you are selling and want to buy it.

Keep it light

You can keep it light and post fun articles. This means that you add in funny pictures or taglines so that your audience can have a laugh. Not everything should be viewed from the point of view of selling your products and promoting your brand. There can be some things that will tickle a funny bone and make them like whatever you have put out. Pick something that will be a hit with a majority of the populace and not something that only a small group will relate to.

Memes

You surely don't want to get left behind and must incorporate as many memes as possible. These memes should be relevant to your content. It is a good idea to Photoshop your products or services within the existing memes and make it look unique and special. You can also make use of a meme generator tool that will help you generate a unique meme. That will be exclusive to your brand. Encourage your audience to share the meme as much as possible.

These are just some of the things that you can do to take full advantage of your Facebook marketing. It is, however, not limited to just these and there are many other things that you can do to make your Facebook marketing campaign grow.

Key highlights

Facebook is by far the most popular social networking site in the world. Since its founding in 2004, it has grown in massive volume over the years. Facebook remains to be the biggest social networking site in the world and will continue to remain that way for a long time to come.

Although it started off as a means for people to keep in touch with each other, Facebook managed to turn into a marketing tool for many companies and individuals alike.

Companies quickly identified the potential that Facebook has in terms of reach and how they can successfully reach out to a large audience. These companies understood what it takes to get noticed by thousands of people all over the world and put in efforts to usher their marketing campaigns into the right direction.

Facebook is popular not just because of its reach but many other reasons as well. It is very easy to operate Facebook and you can get started with it in no time at all. It is easy for your audience to share the posts and other aspects that you share on your site. Facebook allows you to post something new on a daily basis and keep your pages as updated as possible.

You have to get used to the different aspects of Facebook such as the like and share options. These options need to be used to your advantage. You have to make the initial effort of getting as many likes for you page as possible as that can catapult the popularity of your page. Next, you have to know to use both the like and share options in such a way that they help you connect with your audience better. You have to get as many people to share the pages as possible in order to promote your Facebook page.

The posts that you post all need to conform to certain basic standard requirements. If they do not, then they might not do well. For example, the word count must not exceed a certain number and the picture to text ratio should remain within a prescribed limit etc. You have to bear all this in mind when you wish to make the most of your Facebook advertising campaign.

We looked at the different Facebook only offers that you can offer to your customers in order to keep them hooked. It is a great idea for you to use the offers as a means to promote your products exclusively on Facebook and separate it from the rest of the social media programs. You can turn to other exclusive offers as well and not limit it to just the ones mentioned in this book. You can think up other such deals and offers as well and make it a part of your Facebook campaign.

Don't forget to include the call to action request on all your posts. It might sound a bit silly to spoon feed your audience but might be necessary. You have to explain to them what they have to do in order for them to complete the action. If you think they will automatically do it without you expressly telling them then they will not. You should put in requests to help them take notice and do something that you want them to.

Facebook provides a lot of opportunities to companies where they can help it grow in size and reach. You can start by creating a Facebook account for yourself first, in case you don't have one already.

Next, you create a page for your company that will act as your vessel to communicate with your customers. You can follow the step by step procedure to get started with pages and create a unique and interesting one. The page can be customized to your liking and you can help it resonate your individual style.

You can hire a team to take care of your Facebook page. They can keep it up and keep posting content that will appeal to your audience. While hiring a team, you have to look into certain aspects and ensure that they do justice to both your company and the products that you offer to your customers. Remember that it should be a team effort and not an individualistic campaign. You and your creative team should be on the same page when it comes to the ideas that will be used for the campaign. You must give them proper guidance and can hold educative seminars every now and then for them to understand it better.

You have to develop certain Facebook marketing habits that will help you make the most of your marketing efforts. As you know, marketing on Facebook should be viewed as an extremely important aspect of your advertising campaign and something that needs to be taken very seriously. You can go through the specific chapter again if you like in order to understand it better.

We also read on the pitfalls that you have to avoid. Avoiding pitfalls is just as important as developing good habits. These pitfalls can pull you down and so, it is important that you avoid them at all costs.

It is a myth that b2b businesses cannot campaign on Facebook. You should understand that these businesses will have to adopt a unique style when it comes to appealing to their audiences. We looked at some of the different things that businesses can do and why it is important for them to develop and maintain a unique strategy.

We looked at 45 unique Facebook strategies that you must bear in mind while beginning your Facebook campaign. You can go through them once again as each one will help you better your campaign in its own way.

Conducting the customer identification process can help you find the right candidates for your campaign. Once you know who your target audience is, you can come up with campaigns that will succeed. You can divide them based on the different categories to make it easier for yourself.

The Facebook only campaigns can all be used to attract and maintain a large audience on the media. You have to hide certain elements behind the "like" button such as a free coupon that they can cash in on by liking your Facebook page.

Paid advertising is a great concept that you can make use of. It involves buying yourself an audience who can aid in catapulting your business. Paid advertising is generally seen as a bad idea but it is most definitely not one. You can improve your reach considerably by choosing to indulge in it. The process is simple and will leave you with the desired result.

You have to make use of both AdSense and adwords in order to capitalize upon your page's popularity. Both of these will help you earn a good profit which can serve as your parallel or supplementary income. AdSense and adwords are quite smart and will effortlessly do the job for you. You don't have to run behind advertisers, as Google will take care of all the dirty work for you. You can get started with affiliate marketing in the form of AdSense and adwords in no time at all.

Patience is a virtue when you wish to get Facebook pages to work for you. You have to remain patient and not get ahead of yourself especially while starting out. You should remain consistent with your efforts and not allow your interests to dwindle.

CONCLUSION

As you can see, Facebook is very great platform for promoting your brand or business because not only is it powerful, its also very nimble or flexible. Regardless of the nature of your business or brand, Facebook gives you so many options for marketing and promoting them, which allows you to customize your marketing campaigns in terms of budget, time and audience, among others.

All good things worth doing can take time to master – and Facebook marketing is no exception. However, it's worth the time and effort you'll put into mastering it if only for the immense marketing potential for your business or brand.

Because early birds get the worm, businesses that beat most others to the Facebook marketing draw enjoy a huge advantage. As such, it's best for you to strike while the Facebook marketing iron's still hot and be among the early birds! The more entrepreneurs and companies get in on the bandwagon, the more competition you'll have and the lower your chances for successfully marketing your business or brand become.

So what are you waiting for? Start now!

Thank you for Reading! I Need Your Help...

Dear Reader,

I Hope you Enjoyed "**Facebook: Master Facebook Marketing - Facebook Advertising, Small Business & Branding**". I have to tell you, as an Author, I love feedback! I am always seeking ways to improve my current books and make the next ones better. It's readers like you who have the biggest impact on a book's success and development! So, tell me what you liked, what you loved, and even what you hated. I would love to hear from you, and I would like to ask you a favor, if you are so inclined, would you please share a minute to review my book. Loved it, Hated it - I'd just enjoy your feedback. As you May have gleaned from my books, reviews can be tough to come by these days and You the reader have the power make or break the success of a book. If you'd be so kind to CLICK HERE to review the book, I would greatly appreciate it! Thank you so much again for reading "**Facebook: Master Facebook Marketing - Facebook Advertising, Small**

Business & Branding" and for spending time with me! I will see you in the next one!

Check Out More From The Publisher...

Twitter: Master Twitter Marketing - Twitter Advertising, Small Business & Branding

By Grant Kennedy

http://www.amazon.com/Twitter-Marketing-Advertising-Business-Branding-ebook/dp/B01C7SF8JK/

Instagram: Master Instagram Marketing - Instagram Advertising, Small Business & Branding

By Grant Kennedy

http://www.amazon.com/Instagram-Marketing-Advertising-Business-Branding-ebook/dp/B01C3FJJY2/

SEO: Marketing Strategies to Dominate the First Page

by Grant Kennedy

http://www.amazon.com/SEO-Marketing-Strategies-analytics-optimization-ebook/dp/B01ACB7LQM